Kitchens At Night
Dean Browne

smith|doorstop

the poetry business

Published 2022 by
Smith|Doorstop Books
The Poetry Business
Campo House,
54 Campo Lane,
Sheffield S1 2EG

Copyright © Dean Browne 2022
All Rights Reserved

ISBN 978-1-914914-04-1
eBook ISBN 978-1-914914-05-8
Typeset by The Poetry Business
Printed by People for Print, Sheffield

Smith|Doorstop Books are a member of Inpress:
www.inpressbooks.co.uk

Distributed by NBN International, 1 Deltic Avenue,
Rooksley, Milton Keynes MK13 8LD

The Poetry Business gratefully acknowledges
the support of Arts Council England.

Contents

7	Aide-mémoire
8	Curriculum Vitae
9	Memory is a Wardrobe
10	Rachael's Coat Inside Out
11	Pine Box in the Flea Market
13	Quiche
14	Pinball
15	The Goatfish
16	The Émigré
17	The Pineapple Massage
18	Tabernacle
19	Polyphemus
20	Approach to Chilli
21	The Triangle
22	Approach to an Egg
23	Barmbrack
24	My Last Consultation
26	Eclectus
27	Fado With Garlic Crusher
28	Listening to Joni Mitchell's *Blue* While Cooking Peposo
29	Self-Checkout

A storm piles up behind the house.
  – *Elizabeth Bishop, 'Squatter's Children'*

I think a bird, and it begins to fly.
  – *Theodore Roethke, 'The Exulting'*

Aide-mémoire

A goat has been following me for hours. There is a sign
hung around his neck that reads NEVER FORGET.
That's not very original I think but I'll see where it leads.
'I have no grá for you goat,' I say, and clap my hands, say, 'Go!'
His goat eye asks if I am half cracked. 'Grand,' I say,
and keep walking. He follows at a discreet distance, beard
jigging crooked as he jaws blankly at some grass he cropped
years ago, I suppose. What am I meant to remember?
Leaves are smeared on the street, a salad of dragged newspaper.
Nobody appears to notice what is following me. I detour
into a dive bar, roll a cigarette, drink a double whiskey
and try to decide where, if anywhere, all this might connect.
Goat stands by the door, NEVER FORGET dripping to the tiles.
I watch wet leaves fibrillate outside the window, think
of the small, delicate feather on this morning's egg. Leaf, light,
leaf, light. Quick silverfish glimpses of a freedom that spooks
on approach. The goat chews on, relentless. I mash my cigarette,
touch my ear, and it comes off.

Curriculum Vitae

after Charles Simic

I'm demonstrating the excellence of this potato peeler
to an audience who could well be allergic to spuds.
I'm playing the glass harp dressed head to toe in carrageen moss
with a tin can for coins and peculiar weather in my sock.

That's why the daffodil in my buttonhole has that drastic look.
That's why I keep a baseball bat by the bedpost.
I stand around incongruous as party glitter on a coffin lid
with my inevitable questions: *mustard, or ketchup?*

Ah to be hang gliding over the Cork and Kerry mountains –
the going so smooth, it could be sponsored by
a sports drink. That's not a living it's a spaceship, baby.
Still the anxiety persists like an immoderate flugelhorn

and every day's a busted longing somewhere and a boss
like, Withero, catch this monkey.

Memory is a Wardrobe

— *Gaston Bachelard,* The Poetics of Space

I had the blue suitcase open on the floor,
packed cardboard boxes. I thought of Rimbaud's *Le Buffet*,
that scuffed oak wardrobe, how it opened up to him
like an old woman lost for words, tongue torn between
come in / clear off. I'm standing at the wardrobe
now, as though turning the next page
in a good crime novel, and want to sleuth for clues—
follow up that suggestion of perfume or fruit,
that all too often escapes me in seconds, back to
something like contentment for once. I mean, again.
There must be a shoebox of marbles, duelling cards
still buried at the back, beyond the stiff shirts
whispering to each other of the stranger, set adangle
on wire hangers. And beneath them, two drawers that
bruise inwards with the shadow of rich red wine.
I knew this woman who'd shut her larkspur-blue eyelids,
tilt head back, the better to see detail bleeding from
a story. I close my eyes, and some version of the poem
returns: *It's some rush, this interior wilderness ...*
But I forget the rest. The poem disappears in its edition
between others that walk straight through to the sunlight
over the hills, and it clicks that home is where the hurt
is, or has been, or will be.
                           No buffing the blunt scuffs
from its scarred face, the wardrobe. But I know
it knows a thing or two though it's not letting on
when I open back the sly doors and it whistles.

Italicised lines are from my own version of Arthur Rimbaud's poem 'Le Buffet'. This poem is commonly translated as 'The Sideboard'.

Rachael's Coat Inside Out

i.m.

It's floating on a wire hanger now
from the lowest branch in a corner
of the forest. You unhook it,
thumbs worrying stitches for what
you missed last time in the dark
shifty material lining the interior—
the slit left by a torn-away button,
burns, the nervous designs of moths
flickering in and out at the collar.
Your dreams make all kinds of no sense—
locked cabinets with cobwebs across
the wobbly glass knobs. Rachael
adjusts on her nothing shoulders
the winter coat she'd have worn,
the stitching so gone in the pockets
her hands believe they're bottomless.
She could keep a rat in one, the teeth,
the pink loop of tail, brush against us
this close, and who would even know
what she carried there?

Pine Box in the Flea Market

The japanned pine box
with its cold brass handle and clasp
makes an enigma of the room.
Opening it will be intimate, you think –
like the sudden glimpse of a heel
when she nips to the bath
leaving you and the bedposts to interpret
this new hush.

The box is burnished orange brown,
a finish the tint of Chilean myrtle
or something choked with paprika,
with corners that could cut
like fishhooks. Watch your thumbs.
You want to poke about inside,
to shuck it open with an oyster knife,
spy in over the pine horizon,
and *whisht* you're saying *whisht*—

Inside? Maybe a bunch of shrunken heads;
a rosary of goats' teeth, bone blushing;
a pair of rusty, rubber-handled pliers;
the peekaboo of a tarantula—
you are a horsefly learning immensity
at the brink of a donkey's ear.

You can just picture shouldering it home
past bleeding candles, black veils,
mourners falling into step
and the shops closing on MacCurtain Street.
Someone clips a leash on his dog.

This is the clock's insomnia now—
your shoulder killing you all the way home
to a room on a numberless avenue
where blue snow is falling

Quiche

Pain is a basement café and all of us are scrubbing
our merciless scrub, said the lady in the bloody apron,
looking through me. I'd asked for a slice of quiche
with goat's cheese and my finger was frozen on the sneezeglass.

Either I can be your mentor or you can wear pyjamas
the mechanic yelled over the racket in his garage
when I suggested egg white was no substitute for glue.
He climbed under the hood, and hasn't come out since.

A fly on the wall is enough company for a lifetime
my mother insisted, while I stood above her on a stool
tending that fuse box. She wore black all the time now.
She kept spilling Lucozade on the dachshund in her lap.

I was out in the shed, reaching back to oil the hinges
that held my wings in position. It was hot work.
The last hour will be our worst, my wife said, and when I soared
our children were quick red ants leading her from the scene.

Pinball

for Matthew Sweeney

He let the oxygen mask slip
from the crow's nest of stubble
so I leant in closer, to catch
that he didn't want a headstone –
no wings, no spidery gothic script –
instead, an old pinball machine
should mark the place of his grave.
He liked the plink under his thumbs;
he talked bumpers, flippers, kickers,
forbidden tilts, 'shooting for the moon',
how a ball knocked out of bounds
might come back, Lazarus, and win.
I saw tournaments among the tombs,
a horsebox paused by the fresh earth,
a generator, set up to the side
under that knuckle of hill in Donegal.
He inserts the first cold coins
by the yew trees, under the moon,
pulls the plunger—flashing outlanes
bop and spark against the marble,
focusing names and dates,
gilt epitaphs and stone angels
watching hi-scores rack up.
I know before the night is out
his initials will join the wizards'.

The Goatfish

Tired of the new quiet and a cat hair
in the soup you never made as sweet as hers,
at the first cindery pipsqueak of dawn
you'll bestir yourself out into the woods
and live on robins' eggs and rainwater
from a stoup of birch bark, wrung from moss;
chanterelles, brandy-warm, in a lee of ash.
Like wandering Aengus, or like Orpheus
riffing under earth just to double the grief –
this thought teasing at your temples:
as though she might shake off soil and roses,
reappear, mobled in veils, glowing like foxfire,
visible from parish to sister parish, say:
the cut of you, la, and cups left in the sink?
Pack it in, Aengus, Orpheus, pipe down!
The world is more wide for your wandering.
Folding one sock into the other, or
kneeling to separate helm from rhubarb helm
in a straw hat, your ordinary is so strange
you might as well be filleting goatfish
on the far side of the moon – scraped scales
flying from you like a rash of Leonids. La.

The Émigré

'A little / nomadic night at home'
  — James Tate, 'Honey, Can You Hear Me?'

Upturn the bucket of sand on the bedroom floor and spread your fingers
in the ground shell and sea glass—right up to your wrists
until you've shaped a beach between the skirting board and bookcase.
Tape down tarpaulin cut from your old tent tacky with pine sap and pour
the plastic bottle of salt water in the hollow for the sea.
Crêpe crimped at specific points, scored with a pin and suspended
by a shoelace from the ceiling will represent the seagull.
A clipping from your poppy red scarf will represent the crab,
a raw egg, jellyfish—step on it barefoot, there is no pain.
Next sow the tiny fishing boats along the shore: stove in,
windows streaked as if with tears, the starboards like scratch cards—scrape

gunge away with your fingernail and find a girl's name – *Grace*
or *Kate S 609*, a goitre tangled squid-like in the fishnets.
Spark up your last cigarette—do not burn the gull. You can be patient
or you can be patient. Soon a vessel will advance to the shallows.
Catch the captain's eye, and, if he knew your father, he'll ferry you across
that brief body of water to the island on the other side—where,
at low tide, you can unscrew mussels from stone; watch them nose
from their doors, poached in a saucepan with herbs and *Marqués de Riscal*.
You'll watch from a rock the chickens poking around in the seaweed –
russet feathers pearled with spray, eyes freaked a fierce sea-green –
the rosa rugosa, the seals, until one silver hair shows in your fringe.

The Pineapple Massage

after 'ASMR Binaural Pineapple Relaxation', Ephemeral Rift

This YouTube video of a guy massaging a bespectacled pineapple
with jokeshop nose, brushing its spiny leaves and knocking   *hello*

hello tension hello recurrent twinge in the joint outcha come –
he whispers nothings to the fruit, whose day has been so long.

I've never seen food used like this and the algorithm knows –
the dry leaves crickle, he can feel doors opening in the rind

and it's as if I have slipped through one and listen from inside.
I am alone. Oh, I might have laughed at this before:

somewhere there is a man who comforts the people by means
of a pineapple. He schools the ear in his curriculum of touch.

Yeah, even when he produces that big kitchen knife and carves
past the leafy plume to consume his client chunk by chunk –

so the blade sinks inches from my ear and the air brightens
yellow with the summer pent inside and is palpable.

Tabernacle

Castaways, we hit the forest—our camping stove
turned low, I gripped the tent close for its trial
in virgin attitudes of stiffness while
lamps fluttered on the dark. My roof sank wave
on wave accordion-like, the only sin
we knew; and soon the Jameson appeared.
I'd burned one back and by the third
she laid her hand on mine, like a napkin ...

Later, I caught those tiny gasps from Joan
and Michael's tent where he slipped into her
like (this I thought) a frog à la Bashō;
those dark rippling walls where she kept centre,
held her breath, so I had to puzzle how
one could leave and neither be alone.

Polyphemus

He remembers the telescope most on winter nights —
a cheapish starter model, this, but it let him go
to Mare Imbrium and back in minutes;
then he's that nine-year-old who wheels it to the window,
tunes the sky, finds this keyhole in the hemisphere.
Sometimes the lens reflects only his myopic squints,
trained on whatever might chance to constellate
especially for his look — the soft blur
of the Pleiades, or Cassiopeia
he liked to picture rocking on a blue veranda;
or that god who, deaf to his charades, hints
nothing of himself and declines to comment
and is nobody's business for the moment
unless he means to say *Sorry, you're too late.*

Approach to Chilli

I'm catching the back garden in a colander held up
to the kitchen window—catching, rather, the fierce green glare
that filters in. When I've had enough I turn, think
if I took a hacksaw and cut up the kitchen table
piece by piece, at what point exactly would it cease

to *be* a table? Which leg if any contains essence of table?
This kills time. Soon you will be home from a late shift
and I'll have cooked us both a vicious chilli, spitting
with onion, tomato, the red and yellow peppers, lentils, beans,
dashed with paprika, cumin … too much habanero.

Now they're mingling, ready to have their tantrum
on our tongues. What's left but to uncork a *Côtes du Rhône*
and rearrange the sitting room, in my head? There is no
TV, so all the furniture points to the furniture.
I slug back a glass then, one by one, tip up the chairs.

The Triangle

I should never have written the instruction manual
illustrating the 52 distinct tones that can be struck
from the triangle, popular now in concert halls
from here to Berlin. It's brought me nothing but success.

The joke, at first, was exquisite as a devilled egg
and the expression on their faces like a sweet pimento.
You put the phony in symphony tonight, grinned back
the shiny hand dryer in the gents. Gobs dropped

and I went on, describing the point tapped just so
for the blackbird's dawn trill, the ripple on a clear lake
in Sweden, the squeak of gas that jets from a burning coal.
One tone only audible to toddlers, another only to dogs.

Of course I reddened when those rich fools googled me,
the search results proved it true. The hits were legion.
Not only that, the book had entered its fourth print run
and was forthcoming in Russian and Nynorsk.

That's when it occurred to me that I was late
to deliver the keynote address at the annual summit
for lovers of the triangle, my lecture on the sweeter octaves
of beryllium copper – how to damp it for the rustle

like the train of a bridal dress trailed over cobbles.
Or pitch it like the mice celebrating the owl's demise
by lightning, or the *ting!* so crystalline it's called frost creeping.
So I jotted some notes, grabbed my jacket, and said *taxi*.

Approach to an Egg

A boiled egg is a fresh beginning
and you tap the pale frangible shell
so delicately with the edge
of your spoon, you could be a convict

careful not to wake your cellmate
while you test the walls for weak spots,
brow glazed in response to a sun
rising the other side.

Barmbrack

Mother of God,
two houseflies were making love
on what must have been their honeymoon.
My grandmother struck them with a dishcloth.
The dirty fuckers, she said,
sweeping them into her open palm
like currants fallen from the barmbrack loaf
at the heart of which lay a golden ring.

My Last Consultation

Doctor, I give you the bruised fruit
of my torso. Touch and I will dent,
form an ugly brownish hollow. Tap
my knee for a reflex it will fly off
on adventures, barbacking in Prague,
torturing a rival's orchids, a silvery
flick of studded football boot by night,
heeling a white horse over the meadows,
crushing glass at a Jewish wedding, toeing
lifts on the motorway, a nomad, ankleflash …
Doctor, I'm just cheesewire you manipulate
to secure from ravenous, imagined foxes
your next omelette. It is raining in Cork,
in Dublin it is raining, one umbrella is
as effectual as five. Doctor it is raining
in my body. You'll catch your death.
Press your stethoscope to my chest,
do you not hear Bach's Partita No. 2
in D minor as performed inside a whale?
Doctor, I know, I know, I know …
Don't hang all my baskets on one egg.
Don't put all my widgets in one fish.
I will mind the platform between the train
and the gap when I disembogue.
But nine stitches is not so much?
Doctor, I'm tired of this diaphanous façade
of hope but I am not ready yet
to do the obituary mambo. Every job
I've known has been take the shift
or get the shaft. I'm learning to shirk.

But managers haunt, with tall orders,
targets and figures, the imagination.
My anxiety is a born lepidopterist
and my colours flutter in the suffocating
cone of its palms, such a dusky capture
making ash of what was brightest in me.
Doctor, please do not prescribe Rilke.
I ask for your medical not your moral counsel.
When one poodle died, Schopenhauer
would replace it with a new poodle.
To each poodle he gave the same name:
Benedict Cumberbatch.
Doctor, put a name on this dog.
I ask for your scalpel not your scapulars.
You may think you are the donkey's monocle
but you are not even nunchucks.
You may think you are the glistening satin
on a radish, but your cow burns down
while you whisper sweet nothings to milk.
How soon sweet nothings turn
to snickersnee. Doctor, you're bleeding.
Your parrot's clearly microwaved.
It's more chichi than rococo, I agree.
Have you ever wondered, is it art?

Eclectus

What starts it is the Eclectus parrot, named Hannah,
her free-range cock-eyed hop along Wolfe Tone Square,
her unlikely garb of crimson affecting smart casual –
'what business has live poultry doing here?' –
and for once it occurs to me I should ring the father.
We both own phones, do we not? Yet the dead line
fans out between us like an aspirant sapling,
screening each from the other these last few years.
His chicken coops have come down with a lazy shower
of cherry blossoms. See him unlatch the flights, stoop
through low doors, dish seeds, chopped pomegranate
and nuts to the birds he breeds, their feathers hi-vis,
eyes live wired. *Violet is a mutation of blue* he says
and his prized Indian ringnecks strut their genes.
The father is offering glosses on *cleartails, lacewings*, all
I hear are the words. Grateful one of us is speaking.
See him touch the flushed, mango plumage of a sun conure,
a black-headed caique he calls 'the Republican', perched
on his shoulder. Welsummers, rosellas, frilled bantam silkies
need him. One parrot glows foxfire green. The father
reaches in and it shuffles onto his open palms, enters
mine, to my surprise and its. See my thumbs cup the wings
as though this one thing might be kept good between us.

Fado With Garlic Crusher

I opened the shampoo and a swarm of locusts came out.
No problem. I'd gone without before. Be grateful, I said.
I was returning to work finally. I reached into my coat pocket
and had my hand bitten by the tiniest gold-skinned bear
I'd ever seen. I shrugged, I probably deserved it,
I mean there must have been signs missed. I nursed
the bleeding fingers in a napkin I'd kept from our last
trip to the pizzeria by the canal. I disembarked from
the empty train at my usual stop, emerging into the dust
at street-level. The day was fine, some flirting pigeons
dispersed, a woman was playing a mandolin up a tree,
some slow dirge. I'm sure it's happened to somebody somewhere
before. I looked around. The crowds seemed not to notice.
I was two minutes late for work. My boss was delighted.
Yeah right. What time is it? he said. Nine, I said. No,
he said, it's two minutes past. O, I pretended surprise.
I described all that had occurred to me that morning and
was sacked on the spot. 'It's only reasonable, I suppose.'
At least I'd have more time for myself. I gazed at the clouds.
There was something they tried to communicate in their frayed,
drifting formations. I decided to visit our former apartment,
pack the last of my things. She'd left so little, and yet
I expected her to enter any minute, association being
what it is. I handled the garlic crusher, and the sadness
overcame me in great waves. Then I was ravenous,
so I sat down on my suitcase with the last dripping wedge
of melon she'd freshly cut open, about a week before.

Listening to Joni Mitchell's Blue *While Cooking Peposo*

More paint than accompaniment, your chords,
the day I held the yellowed Tuscan recipe
I'd chanced on, bent over charity shop shelves
in Bantry square. Your voice arose from blue –
I mean my Bluetooth pocket speaker, Spotified –
queued and looped and ringing fine as glass.
You say: *the bed's too big, the frying pan's too wide*
but here is a shell for the blue. Who's Richard?
All ears, I seared cubed beef with garlic cloves,
a teacup of Chianti, black pepper in reckless dashes –
I chopped tomatoes gorgeous as her mouth
that sea-lit evening. And, though she didn't stay,
still your voice moves through my kitchen at night.
It's 'California': *Will you take me as I am.*

Self-Checkout

He told me he got lost once
in the aisles of a Tesco Express –
not physically disorientated,
more as if a glitch occurred
in the escapement of a timepiece –
a wheel the size of a coffee bean
scooting loose, and all gravity
pressed down on that space.

All the apples fell there.
I think I know what he meant.
He'd left the gaff for celery
not an existential bruhaha.
Some days I know myself
only in the way you'd consume
a crisp green apple, keeping
distance from the core.

It is necessary to remember
the hardy grain of the table
in a kitchen in Aherlow,
how it spoke to your elbows:
I was once a seed
so minute you could swallow me
whole and not notice.
Lean on me, be nourished.

Acknowledgements

Thanks to the following publications where some of these poems have previously appeared: *Banshee, Bath Magg, Poetry Ireland Review, The Poetry Review, POETRY, Southword, The Stinging Fly, The Tangerine.*

'My Last Consultation' was winner of The Geoffrey Dearmer Prize, 2021.

'Pine Box in the Flea Market' was shortlisted for the Irish Book Awards Poem of the Year, 2019.

I'm indebted to the Arts Council of Ireland for vital support during the completion of this work, as well as the Tipperary County Council for a Tipperary Artists Award, 2021.

Sincere thanks to Ann and Peter Sansom at Smith|Doorstop for their editorial guidance and belief in the work.

For support at various points I'm grateful to: Ben Burns; Philip Cremin; Crónán Ó Doibhlin; Michael Dooley; Cal Doyle; Shane Forde; Don Hanley; Scott McKendry; John Mee; Tom Moore; Gerry Murphy; Mary Noonan; Billy Ramsell; Maurice Riordan; Stephen Sexton; Matthew Sweeney; Jessica Traynor; Brian Turner.

Thanks also to Patrick Cotter of The Munster Literature Centre, Cork, and to Paul Casey of O'Bheal.

Thanks to my parents and my grandmother Margaret, 'Mum'.

My love to Laura.